Learning A

by Tristan F. Nicholas

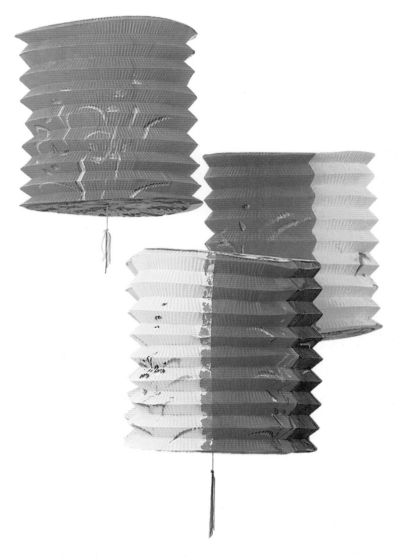

PEARSON
Scott
Foresman

What gives off heat?

Heat moves from warm
things to cool things.
Heat comes from the light of the Sun.
Light from the Sun warms Earth.

Heat

Heat comes from fire.

Heat makes things warm.

Heat comes from other things too.

What can energy do?

Light is a kind of energy.
Light from the Sun is energy.
Energy can change things.
It can change something from
cold to hot.

Dark colors take in a lot of light.
Light colors take in less light.
Things with light colors feel cooler.

What makes light and shadows?

Light comes from the Sun.

Light comes from fire too.

Light comes from stars and candles.
Light even comes from this bug!
Where else does light come from?

Making Shadows

Things can block light.
Toys block light.
Shine the light
on the toy.
A shadow
is made.

Shadows are made when things block light.

The shadow is big when the light is close.

The shadow is small when the light is far away.

Changing Shadows

Shadows can change.
A tree makes a shadow in the morning.

The tree makes a different shadow at noon.
Shadows change when the Sun seems to move.

What uses energy around us?

Fuel is something that is burned.

It is burned to make heat or power.

Gasoline is a fuel.

A car burns gasoline.

Electricity makes things work.

Lights use electricity.

Using Energy

A fan gets energy from electricity.

Plug in the cord.

The toy gets energy from a battery.

A **battery** stores energy.

How do you get energy?

You use energy all the time.

You get energy from food.

Energy helps you move and grow.

Glossary

battery   something that stores energy

electricity   makes some things work

energy   can change things

fuel   anything that is burned to make heat or power

heat   moves from warmer places and objects to cooler places and objects

shadow   made when something blocks the light